"Never begin an important design project unless you have had at least eight hours' sleep followed by a nutritious breakfast."

Mao Tse-Tung

2

Graphic Design as a Second Language

Bob Gill

Published in Australia in 2003 by
The Images Publishing Group Pty Ltd
ACN 059 734 431
6 Bastow Place, Mulgrave, Victoria 3170, Australia
Telephone (61 3) 9561 5544 Facsimile (61 3) 9561 4860
Email: books@images.com.au
Website: www.imagespublishinggroup.com

National Library of Australia Cataloguing-in-Publication Data

Gill, Bob.
Graphic Design as a Second Language

ISBN: 1 920744 39 8

1. Graphic arts.
2. Graphic design (typography). I. Title.

Design: Bob Gill
Digital artwork: Jack Gill
Pre-press: Christine Cirker
Printed by Max Production Printing & Book-binding Limited

IMAGES has included on its website a page for special notices
in relation to this and our other publications. It includes updates
in relation to the information printed in our books. Please visit
this site: www.imagespublishinggroup.com

4

Contents

1 Definitions 7
Design, Problem/Solution, Statement, Concept,
Idea, The culture, Inevitability, Vocabulary, Collage,
Montage, Repitetion, Parody, Distortion, Continuity

2 An overview 21
Special effects, Reality, The computer

3 Design lite 27
Unnaturalness, Internal logic, Separation, The grid,
Natures "ungrid", Consistency/variety
Typography condensed, Redundancy

4 Process 37
The brief, The problem is the problem,
Research, Listening, Exaggeration, Less is more.
More is also more.

5 Connections 55

6 Found objects 65

7 Clichés 73

8 Word as word 81

**9 Letterform and
word as image 85**

10 On the other hand... 91
Impossible images, Paradox, Abstraction

11 Other voices...other ways 107
Rene Magritte, Muller Brockmann, Saul Steinberg,
Ramond Savinac, David Carson, Karel Martens,
Karl Gerstner, Franco Grignani, Bruno Munguzzi.

12 Coda 113
Theory, practice

13 Credits, clients, bio 121

6

1. Definitions

Let's begin by defining some terms so that the reader will know precisely what I mean when I use them, as applied to graphic design.

Design

Design is way of organizing something.

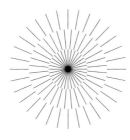

See page 100.

You cannot hold design in your hand. It is not a thing. It is a process. A system. A way of thinking.

There's no such thing as "good design" or "bad design." The design is good if it does what you want it to do. It's bad if it doesn't.

In order to have a design, you need something to organize.

Problem/Solution

What has to be organized, I call the *problem*.

Design is the *solution*. This means that design can only be evaluated, (be judged good or bad), if you know what the design is *supposed* to organize. What it is supposed to accomplish.

That's why there are no absolutes in design. Any rules or truths that you may have picked up about design, color, balance, etc., are valid only if they help you accomplish what you wish. Otherwise, forget them.

There are no colors or typefaces or layouts or images that are *always* good. Or *always* bad.

Graffiti is often an eyesore. But as I was thinking about an ad announcing a film about teenage gangs in Los Angeles, I noticed a truck covered in graffiti. It seemed so right as an image of violence and nihilism.

I photographed the truck and added the title of the film.

A very crude, cheap device for stamping out letters is called *Dymo*. By any standards, its about the lowest form of typography.

So, I guess that's bad. But when I had to design a change of address card, I used *Dymo*. The same system that every New York City landlord uses to put the new tenant's name in the slot next to their apartment bell.

A designer who knows what a solution should look like, before he knows the problem, is as ridiculous as a mathematician who knows the answer is 112 before he knows the question.

Statement

You are given a problem: a logo for a dry cleaner. Whatever your solution, it communicates *something*.

If your statement is boring, then chances are that your solution will be boring.

Concept

Please never use the word, concept.

Great thinkers like Einstein and Newton think of concepts like relativity and gravity. And of course, there are film producers and car makers with their dopey concept films and concept cars.

Idea

We, humble graphic designers, *never* get concepts. Only ideas.

And don't confuse an idea with a fact.

For example:

You walk into a classroom. You say, "there are twenty-six chairs in the room." *That's a fact.* Anyone who can count could have said the same thing.

However, if you have a personal opinion about the chairs, and say, "as the chairs are lined up so perfectly, I bet the atmosphere in this room must be very rigid."

That's an idea. Not profound. But an idea.

The ideas you will have, which come from your personal take on every new job, every new experience, largely determine the quality of your graphic design.

If your idea is boring, then chances are that your image will be boring.

The culture

Neil Postman, in his brilliant book, *Amusing Ourselves to Death,* points out that, when 1984 came, we boasted that the ominous prediction by Orwell, in *1984* that we would be enslaved by Big Brother, never happened.

Postman also said, that Aldous Huxley's prediction in *Brave New World,* that "people will come to love their oppression, to adore the technologies that undo their capacities to think," *did come true.*

It's not Big Brother who's watching you, it's Disney and Time/Life and Rupert Murdoch and a few other mega-corporations.

The culture which they inflict on us through their virtual monopoly of television, cable, radio, film, theater, magazines, CDs, etc., is designed almost exclusively, to appeal to the lowest common denominator, which in turn, allows them to sell us the largest amount of stuff. Of course, they allow just enough high culture, to show that they are not Philistines.

And judging from their insatiable appetite to control more and more media, there will probably be even less diversity in the future.

So if you're to become an original thinker, you've must extricate yourself from the mega-corporation's avalanche of white bread.

Inevitability

There's nothing more embarrassing than a juggler who always looks as if he's about to drop whatever he's juggling.

By my standards, however difficult it is to make art, it should always *look* easy, never labored. That's what I mean by inevitable.

After the curtain came down on a Paddy Chayefsky play, the person sitting next to me got up and complained to his wife, "what's the big deal? I cudda written that."

I assumed that what he meant, was that he was not aware of anything the playwright actually *did*. It was as if the playwright simply pressed the *on* button of a tape recorder, so that the play could write itself. The fact that the characters in the play were so convincing, was its *strength*.

This is what I try for. I *like* the idea that if I'm successful, the guy who sat next to me that night, would have the same reaction to my work, as he did with Chayefsky's.

Vocabulary

Once we have an idea, which then suggests a particular image, (say, a banana), we then have to decide how the image is rendered.

Should it be art or photography? If a painting or a drawing, should it be realistic or not? If a photograph, should it be black and white, or in color, or in line or a halftone or a silhouette?

How an image is rendered, should always depend on how it helps express the statement best.

For example:

In this Mother's Day department store internal poster, the mother and child are rendered as a *line photograph.*

In spite of the lack of detail, mother and child are easily recognized.

The line version has the advantage over a halftone photograph of being very graphic and simple.

Instead of showing an *ideal* couple who reads the magazine as in most readership surveys, I decided to go to the other extreme.

The photograph of the couple on the cover of this survey, needs as much detail as possible to appreciate their personalities: that they are the most *unlikely couple* to read the magazine.

Whenever one of my solutions calls for a drawing, I try to use a line that best suits the subject.

This means that I don't have a particular style.

Art directors who give out illustration assignments don't like this, because they never know what I will do.

Neither do I.

Here are three examples:

a mechanical line for the logo of a radio program distributor/producer.

a heavy, sad line to represent the characters in a tragedy.

a light, silly line for a humorous ad.

More vocabulary:

Collage

an assembly of *various* flat visual materials such as paper, cloth, etc. to make a single composition.

The Great American Backrub wishes you a stress-free holiday.

For example:

A company's 17" by 22" mailer, wishing their friends and customers a *stress-free* holiday. The company is ir the *relaxing* business. They give backrubs.

Also, see page 86.

14

Montage

an assembly of the *same* visual material.

For example:

My eleven-year-old daughter, Kate, did this amazing photo montage in school.

Also, see page 93.

Repetition

A single image is okay. But, that sam image, when multiplied a number of times, opposite, is often irresistible.

Parody

A literary or artistic work that makes fun of another work is called a parody.

Problem:
illustration for *Mother's Day.*

I couldn't get the famous Whistler icon out of my mind.

Brought up to date, by painting "mother" waiting for the telephone to ring.

Distortion

Twisting something out of its normal shape, (distorting it) can be a very effective way of dramatizing a visual statement.

Ever since the computer became the graphic designer's standard equipment, distorting an image is as easy as clicking a mouse.

The question is, when to bring in this heavy artillery?

My suggestion: very rarely.

A diary to celebrate the new millennium, consisted of quotations from great thinkers which contradicted each other. (More images from the diary on pages 96 and 97.)

On a left-hand page:
"Like father like son."
R. Rolle

On the right-hand page:
"The child is father of the man."
John Milton

Continuity

In an advertising campaign, or a series of promotional pieces, or a range of packaging, etc., several solutions are needed for, essentially, the same problem.

Each piece has to stand on its own, (be independently interesting), while at the same time, be consistent with the client's "corporate identity" (yesterday's word) "branding" (today word) or (God knows what tomorrow's jargon will be).

For example:

a series of images for an advertising campaign with the theme, *There's no mistaking White Horse Whisky.*

Problem:
two mailers about doing everything from logos to posters to ads to illustrations, etc.

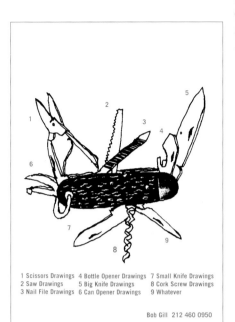

1 Scissors Drawings   4 Bottle Opener Drawings   7 Small Knife Drawings
2 Saw Drawings   5 Big Knife Drawings   8 Cork Screw Drawings
3 Nail File Drawings   6 Can Opener Drawings   9 Whatever

Bob Gill 212 460 0950

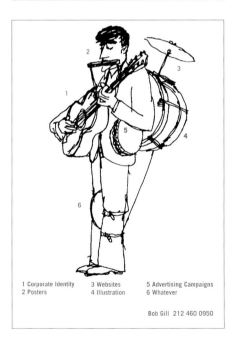

1 Corporate Identity   3 Websites   5 Advertising Campaigns
2 Posters   4 Illustration   6 Whatever

Bob Gill 212 460 0950

Special effects

If you expect to design printed matter, the competition will be from an actor in a film about aliens. He will be endowed with special effects which cost a fortune and are truly dazzling.

And this is only the beginning. By the time you read this, the effects of the next generation of movies will be even more amazing.

The people who will see these movies are the same people who will see your booklet, or your ad for dog food or toothpaste or some other boring product. And your client, naturally, expects these people to be as excited about your work as they were about the special effects in the movie or video.

How can you possibly compete in static print with the animated magic of video and film?

I suggest that there is only one way. You shouldn't be tempted to produce watered-down versions of special effects. You don't have the technology, or the budget or the time.

You should go to the other extreme.

Reality

We have to say to our audience, in effect, "hey, look at this. You've seen this a hundred times. But have you ever noticed it before?"

For example:

Have you ever noticed that when pictures that have been hanging on wall for some time, are removed, they leave marks?

These marks can become a fresh way of saying, "an art gallery has moved."

That, to me, is as interesting as the most spectacular special effects. An more persuasive, because it's true.

The Forum Gallery is moving to
745 Fifth Ave., New York, NY 10151 on December 1, 2001
Tel: 212 355-4545 Fax: 212 355-4547

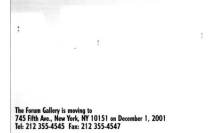

A very ordinary image such as a folded bit of cardboard...

becomes a logo for a company which organizes conferences...

or the scale in the lower right-hand corner of almost every map...

CommunityCartography

becomes the logo for a map-making company...

or a pencil sharpener, with lots of colored shavings becomes a decorative element on a magazine cover...

or a pencil with points at both ends representing two one-act plays.

So, if you are not in the habit of carefully observing everything around you...do it. You'll find that it is an infinite source of useful images and ideas.

There's another thing about the situation today, that designers must recognize...

The computer

Before computers, the production of printed matter was in the hands of designers and printers. Most clients had only the vaguest idea how it was produced. And they were prepared to pay well for their logos, newsletters, annual reports, brochures and other business paper.

But that's not the way it is now.

Now, for a pittance, it's possible to buy a program which allows anyone who can type and has a computer, a printer and a scanner to produce most of the material for the average business.

The mystique has finally gone out of ordinary design and print. Programs fit words and images into professional looking formats. They even throw in some *special effects*.

And all this is adequate for low-end commercial needs.

So, if a typist can do much of the work previously done by well-paid specialists, what's left for the designer? Designers have to do something that a typist with a computer *can't* do.

Designers now have to be problem solvers. They have to be thinkers.

The computer has made the designer's life a lot easier.

No more paste-ups and mechanicals. No more dependency on outside typesetting and photostats. And no more outside photo retouching for most photographic problems.

So far, so good...

However, instead of creating a specific image for a specific job, many designers now browse the various stock shot libraries, that proliferate on the Internet, and can usually find something that *more or less* comes close enough for their idea.

Given the availability of the millions of stock shots, fewer and fewer clients will want to spend that much more on original images.

Even more ominous, is that students seem less and less inclined to draw or photograph their own images, when it's so easy to scan someone else's.

This means that when teachers try to evaluate students' thinking, they're never sure that they're looking at *exactly* what they intended, or the *closest* they could come to represent their idea with someone else's scanned image.

26

3. Design lite

I suppose that in a book about graphic design, I should devote at least a modicum of space to design, in the formal sense.

I hesitate devoting pages to the subject because:

I don't know very much about design principles.

I hated my basic design teacher.

There are, however, a few, you should excuse the expression, principles that I *have* found useful.

However, as I've said before, if these ideas don't work for you, forget them.

The first collection of my work was published in 1985.

Unnaturalness (there isn't such a word, but there should be.)

We can't trust design decisions that *come naturally*.

It is not *natural* to make an image *very* big,

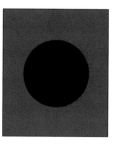

or *very* small,

or *very* dark,

or *very* light.

It's not natural to go to the extreme. But it's the best way to make sure the statement is understood *and* noticed.

Internal logic

The fewer design decisions that seem arbitrary, the better.

Obviously, the client is more likely to accept your suggestions, if they are the best ones to represent the idea, rather than those reflecting your aesthetic prejudices.

Also, if you don't push your personal favorite colors, typefaces, layouts, etc., and you try to do justice to the idea, you might even discover *new* favorite colors, typefaces, layouts, etc.

Separation

The relationship of the elements in a design to each other should be truthful, whenever possible.

For example:

The word "hand" in Fig.1 looks like it is part of the hand. Not true.

The word "hand" in Fig.2 is separate from the hand. True.

True is usually better than not true. (But not always.) See pages 91-105.

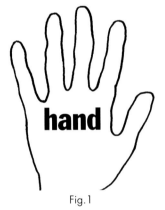

Fig. 1

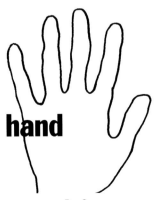

Fig.2

The grid

A system of equally spaced vertical and horizontal lines becomes a useful vehicle to relate typographic and other visual elements in layouts.

The grid is particularly useful when laying out more than one page, where, ideally, we want to vary the pages and at the same time to have the pages relate to each other.

The mathematical connections in the grid are felt, even though the reader doesn't actually measure them.

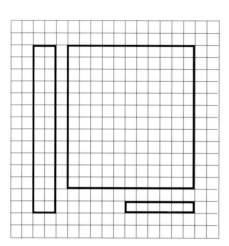

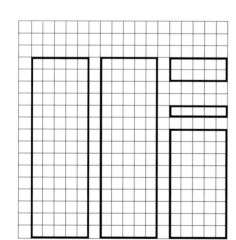

Nature's "ungrid"

Grids are fine. But there are other ways to design. You decide.

Have you ever seen Autumn leaves, after they fall to the ground, arrange themselves in a very boring composition? I haven't.

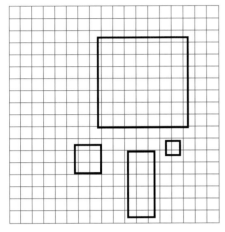

What about pigeons, stopping for a rest in a pavement square? Do they arrange themselves in a boring layout? I've never seen it.

The spatial relationships found in these random, arrangements of leaves or pigeons or almost any natural accidents are never mechanical, or predictable or uninteresting.

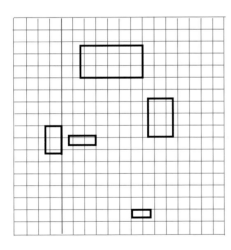

This lesson that nature teaches us is simple, but very important.

Of course, if you prefer to relate the spaces mathematically, go for it.

Otherwise, listen to the pigeons.

Be consistent *and* varied

Ideally, anything that presumes to be creative; choreography, a painting, a waltz, a book jacket, etc., must juggle two seemingly contradictory qualities.

It must not be boring.

And it should hold together as a single entity.

For example:

Problem:
logo for a comedy about a character who gets banged up in an accident. The name of the play is the name of the character.

Solution:
bandaging the name.

HOROWITZ

The design problem:
although each letterform has a different bandage, the whole name should have a consistent look.

Typography: condensed version

Redundancy (too many typographic variations at one time)

Obviously, life would be very boring, without variety. The same holds true with typography. However, *too* much variety is as boring as no variety.

In general, if you vary only one dimension of type, that should give you as much variety as you need.

16 pt. Meta Plus Bold	font
16 pt. Meta Plus Book	weight
16 pt. Meta Plus Bold ital.	style: italic, all caps, underline, etc.
8 pt. Meta Plus Bold	size
16 pt. Meta Plus Bold	color
16 pt. Meta Plus Bold	position

Shape (the best shapes are invisible)

Here's an example:

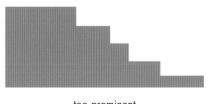

too prominent

**The shape
that the lines of
type make, should
not be more prominent
than the meaning of the words.**

invisible

**The shape that the lines
of type make, should
not be more prominent than
the meaning of the words.**

Redundancy: word/image

Almost every example of graphic design consists of words and images.

Fig. 1

Ideally, it should never be necessary for the words to *tell* us what we are looking at. (Fig. 1) If it *is* necessary, then there's probably something wrong with the image.

Fig. 2

The words should *complement* the image. (Fig. 2)

34

Fig. 1

Fig. 2

Redundancy: scale

The various elements in a layout are either redundant, or complementary.

For example:

The type and the image (Figs. 1 and 2) are either *both* very large or very small. The type and the image compete with each other for the reader's attention.

This is what I call *redundant*.

Fig. 3

Fig. 4

The type is large and the image small. (Fig. 3)

The type is small and the image is large. (Fig. 4)

The reader has no problem knowing which element is most important in Figs. 3 and 4.

This is what I call *complementary*.

36

4. Process

This book is about how the ordinary problems that a graphic designer experiences needn't result in ordinary solutions.

Provided the designer is prepared to let go of any preconceptions about how design is *supposed* to look.

The brief

Your client knows more about what he wants to say about his business than you do. You know more about *how* to say it than he does. If you feel his message is either too complicated or inappropriate for the market, you should discuss it with him.

Remember, there's no future in trying to ram your aesthetic prejudices down his throat. Why should clients have your sensibilities? Your background is in art. Theirs is in commerce.

Eventually, you and your client have to agree on what the problem is, if you are to have any chance to get your solution accepted. Then, at least, when you present your work, there is no doubt that you did exactly what was expected.

There's no use complaining that your brilliant solution was rejected.
That's part of your job: getting your solution *accepted*.

**There's no such thing as a bad client.
There are only bad designers.**

The problem is the problem

Assuming you and your client have agreed upon what is to be communicated, this first step has nothing to do with design. Design has nothing to do with deciding wh the problem is.

Design has also nothing to do with taking the problem, which is invariably boring, and somehow, redefining it, so that it is interesting. That's the second step.

Unless you can begin with an interesting problem, it is unlikely tha you will end up with an interesting solution.

It is only *after* you have changed the problem into an interesting one that thinking about design makes any sense.

Here's an example of changing a boring problem into an interesting one without changing the client's message:

Original problem:
logo for AGM, a company that makes very small models.
(The obvious, boring solution to the obvious boring problem is to do a very small AGM.)

Problem redefined:
logo, when very large, as on the sid of their delivery van, still *seems* very small.

Solution:
regardless of how large the AGM,
put it next to something which shows
that it is small.

Research

When you get a problem, regardless
of how familiar you are with the
subject, resist any temptation to think
you know enough about it, and that
you're ready to begin designing.

Assume that as all of the information
and imagry in your head was put
there by the culture Mafia. None of
the information and imagry is
original with you.

Research the subject, as if you know nothing about it.

If you're doing an ad for, say, a dry
cleaner, don't sit in your studio,
thumbing through design collections,
looking for inspiration, go to a dry
cleaner.

And sit there. Think about dry
cleaning. Ask questions. (Even if the
job isn't about dry cleaning, I might go
there anyway. The naptha fumes are
a trip.)

I don't know exactly what you should
do. I don't have a system which will
guarantee brilliant results. But that's
good. If I had a system, then the
process would become academic
and I would get bored.

Don't be impatient. You'll get there in the end.

How will you know when you have something interesting to say?

If you're honest with yourself, you *will* know. But if you think you're unable to judge if an idea is any good, then perhaps you should think about another profession.

Listen to your idea

Once you have something interesting to say, try and let the statement tell you *how* it should look, regardless of your own visual prejudices.

Here's an example:

Statement:
all woman are whores—all men are sadists, according to the plot of a ballet.

I photographed two dancers from the cast. I cut out the figures and mounted the photographs on cardboard so that they became two-dimensional standing figures. Then I photographed them again...my way of saying that these characters were unreal...that they were stereotypes.

40

Here's another example of how listening to the statement leads to surprising imagry.

Original problem:
poster for a play about a father who goes berserk and murders his young son.

Problem redefined:
how can an image of a father and young son go berserk?

Where is there an image of a father and son that also can become a vehicle for going wild?

Solution:
a child's coloring book.

And then I went wild.

That's the most interesting thing about the process described in this book.

One day, cut-out cardboard figures... another day imitating the kitsch drawings in a children's coloring book.

Ideally, every job...a new experience.

Occasionally, a logo problem
suggests a series of images rather
than a single one.

A Lake Association needed a logo fo
its quarterly newsletter.

This logo changes with the seasons.

Another example of four logos instea
of one for a tie store.

The letterhead, envelope, business car
and invoice each has a different tie.

Problem:
an ecumenical holiday card.
Opposite.

My wife and I have separate letterheads. However, there are time when a joint one would be useful.

Original problem: letterhead for two individuals.

Problem redefined: how can two letterheads be combined into one?

44

Solution: a single, die-cut sheet.

If you can't say something interesting *and* positive about something, at least say something interesting.

Original problem:
jacket for a book with lots of technical information for printers and others in the publishing business.

Problem redefined:
as hard as I tried, I couldn't think of anything positive to say about this monumentally boring book, except that it was heavy.

So I made a dummy book and jacket, put it on an old scale, and weighed it.

Exaggeration

Original problem:
record sleeve for an eccentric jazz pianist. (Remember vinyl—those 12" round things?)

Problem redefined:
what does an *eccentric* record look like?

Solution:
retouching the photograph of a conventional record, so that the grooves are in an eccentric place and persuading the manufacturer to drill a hole in the sleeve, and to put the actual record label on the sleeve.

I had to do an image of the comedians, Bob and Ray on two occasions. The fact that Bob was thin and Ray was fat, suggested the first idea.

The second time I had the same problem, I had some fun with the traditional solution of identifying lots of people in a group photo.

Only this time, it was two people.

1. Bob　　　2. Ray

Original problem:
illustration for the course: "how to get through to *anyone* on the telephone

Problem redefined:
illustration of the most difficult person in the world to reach on the telephone.

46

A poster for a talk I gave about dealing with difficult clients.

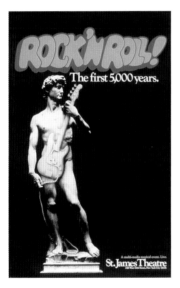

A poster for a live and multimedia history of Rock 'n Roll which I wrote and designed for Broadway, with Robert Rabinowitz, the painter.

While the cast sang all of the rock seminal songs of the first forty years, film and slides surrounded the musicians with the seminal events of the past 5,000 years.

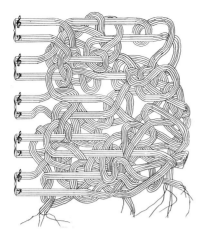

Illustration: jazz
As jazz is improvised music, I began
by drawing the musical staff. And
then I improvised.

Original problem:
logo for a series of radio debates
between liberals and conservatives.

Problem redefined:
express the controversy through the
entangled wires.

Original problem:
illustration in a company brochure
about the availability of its staff, day
and night, seven days a week.

Problem redefined:
how can the company's services be
seen as more available than those c
of the competition…that there wasn'
single business open in the evening
except my client's.

Solution:
an example of what I mean when I
say, "take your idea as far as
possible." Opposite.

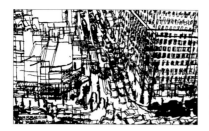

Less is more. More is *also* more.

As a way of illustrating heavy traffic, double-exposed my drawing to show as many cars as possible that could fit in the street.

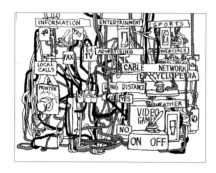

A comment on the *information explosion.*

A cameraman has to carry lots of equipment. Just to make sure that everyone gets the message, I added even *more* stuff in his logo.

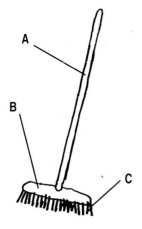

An illustration for a course in how to run an office cleaning business.

The non-technical drawing becomes even sillier with the typeset letters.

An illustration for a course for people who have a problem with ballroom dancing.

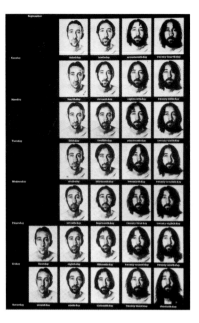

Twelve designers were asked to do one month each of a calendar to be sold for the benefit of a charity.

In thinking about one month, I thoug of exploring growth.

I found the hairiest student that I'd ever seen, and got him to agree to le me photograph him as all of his hair and beard were cut.

And then I arranged the thirty most dramatic photographs in reverse order.

Problem:
moving announcement.

The most interesting image of moving I could think of, was to show every single thing that I was moving; ties, shirts, chairs, table, silverware, pens drawing table, bed, piano, books, shoes, portfolio, toothbrush, food, etc

Having decided that, the next thing was to decide how to *represent* all the stuff.

I ended up with a 17" by 22" announcement with images cut out of a catalog.

Opposite:
an illustration of football violence.

54

5. Connections

Science tells us that everything in our universe is related.

All the more reason to assume that no matter how two parts of a statement *seem* to be unrelated, it should always be possible to find a simple, single image to represent both parts.

Less is more

A typical problem, in that it involves two unrelated subjects:

Television Associates wanted to use the initials, TA as a logo. Instead of trying to do a trendy, graphically exciting monogram, which doesn't communicate anything, I made the problem more interesting:

How can the initials TA also say TV?

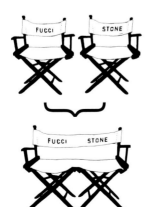

Original problem:
logo for a film production company.

Problem redefined:
logo for a film production company with two partner/directors.

Original problem:
logo for a film about a character wh[o]
tried to seduce every woman he me[t]

Problem redefined:
can a single image communicate th[e]
actor's character?

Original problem:
logo for a series of United Nations
informal luncheons.

Problem redefined:
make a connection between the
formality of the United Nations
and the informality of the luncheons.

What would I have done with a
United Nations informal *breakfast*?

I haven't the slightest idea.

Original problem:
magazine illustration: *working at home.*

Problem redefined:
represent the extreme of both states in one image.

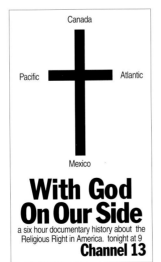

Problem:
newspaper ad for a television program about the growing influence of the *Religious Right.*

Problem redefined:
represent religion's reach from coast-to-coast.

Notice how the more specific the statement, the more likely to result in an interesting solution.

Canada

Pacific   Atlantic

Mexico

**With God
On Our Side**
a six hour documentary history about the
Religious Right in America. tonight at 9
Channel 13

Original problem:
logo for British packaged goods in
international trade fairs.

Problem redefined:
logo which relates the Union Jack
and packages.

Original problem:
an ecumenical holiday card.

Problem redefined:
what do the icons of Christmas and
Chanukah have in common?

Answer:
a fat man with a white beard.

Solution:
inspired by children's paper dolls.

Original problem:
logo for a company that produces
many different sorts of drinks, from
beer to soft drinks, etc.

Problem redefined:
is there a simple image that links *every*
drink?

Original problem:
cover for a fundraising brochure.

Problem redefined:
make a connection between the name
of the organization and fundraising.

Original problem:
television logo for a sitcom about a
secretary.

Problem redefined:
make a connection between the title and
the character of the secretary.

A connection between tourism and
archeological sites in a newspaper a

Original problem:
film logo.

Problem redefined:
A connection between a ruler who
was once adored, and later despisec

Solution:
I got the studio to make a cast of th
head of the star, so I could smash it

Problem:
poster for a three-man photographic exhibition.

Solution:
all three photographers under the camera cloth at the same time.

A connection between a house painter and a student painter in a poster announcing an art school's move.

A film about a boy who delivers secret messages between two lovers.

I had him running in both directions at the same time, by cutting the photograph in half, and flopping the bottom half.

An image of two typical telephone kiosks in an annual report of a company with offices in London and New York.

And in the same annual report, comparing New York and London police.

An image and headline for an ad promoting tourism in Israel which ran in December, in chilly London.

This is a winter coat.

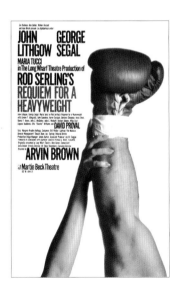

Poster for a play about a failed fighter who is transformed by his lover into a winner.

64

6. Found objects

People have been making images for the past eight million years; x-rays, flags, NASA moon photographs, comic books, paintings on cave walls, theater masks, pub signs, graffiti, Civil War daguerreotypes, engravings, Christmas cards, the *Mona Lisa*, etc.

These images, depending upon how they are used, can transcend their original narrow purpose. They can represent a period of history or a cultural attitude. Or they can symbolize very specific ideas.

If you come across one of these images that says exactly what you want, use it.

For example:

Original problem:
image for an Edwardian comedy about divorce.

Problem redefined:
how can a non-visual idea such as divorce be made visual?

Solution:
an Edwardian print of a patrician couple like the characters in the play.

And then I divorced them.

Recently, as I finished my bacon, lettuce and tomato sandwich on rye toast in the local greasy spoon, the waitress handed me the check.

I looked at it, as if for the first time, although I, and every other New Yorker, have lived with it forever.

I suddenly realized what a fresh invoice it would make.

An expatriot living in Paris needed a letterhead.

I wouldn't presume to improve on the standard French house number plate.

Original problem:
program cover for a piano recital.

Problem redefined:
program cover that, unlike every other one, doesn't have a photograph of the pianist on the cover.

Solution:
represent Rachmaninoff and Gershwin, the two extremes of the program.

Original problem:
announcement that a printer has appointed a design consultant.

Problem redefined:
make a connection between a printer and a non-printer.

Solution:
printers always seem to have ink on their hands.

Two posters to promote a newspaper classified advertising, using ordinary stationery store signs.

68

A five dollar bill and a twenty dollar bill seemed an ideal way to represent the value of twenty-five dollars on a gift certificate.

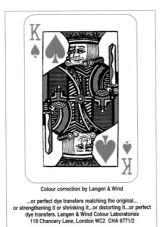

Original problem:
mailing piece for a dye transfer lab promoting their color correcting services.

Problem redefined:
find an image that instantly communicates the *wrong* color.

As each ad appeared in this advertising campaign for The English Designers and Art Directors Association (D&AD), I introduced another standard supermarket image.

The ads were designed to get designers and art directors to submit work for D&AD's annual exhibition.

Problem:
logo for a film project about the history of writing.

Solution:
a classic penmanship image from th golden age of writing.

The Learning Annex Annual Report: 1999

The definitive image of a schoolbook with lots of tabs showing the various courses on the cover of this annual report for a company in the adult education business.

Opposite:
another annual report cover using the standard notebooks

The Learning Annex Annual Report: 2001

Skull and crossbones = pirate
Heart = love
Stars and stripes = America
A sunrise = a fresh start
Magnifying glass = detective

These common images, along with many others, enjoy the advantages of instantaneous communication.

Unfortunately, these clichés are so over used, that they're no longer of any interest.

But, I'm reluctant to promise never to use magnifying glasses or sunrises or other all too familiar images.

There's nothing wrong with using clichés, as long as fresh ways of using them can be found.

Original problem:
logo for a film production company.

Problem redefined:
find a connection between the company's initials, and an instantly recognizable film icon.

I wanted to send a holiday card to friends and clients.

Considering that the tragedy of the World Trade Center happened only a few months before, a gray card seemed right.

You'll laugh, scream, make new friends, have an adventure, eat like a King, be home by 8:30. Incredible Special Price of $84.95 includes Roundtrip Delux Coach. Free Instruction & Guides. Safety Vests & Wet Suits. Six Hour Raft Trip. Light Breakfast. Zabar's Gourmet Lunch. Free Drinks on the Party Bus Going HOme. Tel: (212) 580-2828 for immediate registration

I rewrote the headline of this ad for an inexpensive rafting trip, so that I could use *horror film* lettering.

A classified ad of a logo designer, on the cover of a booklet of logos.

Comic books are a wonderful source of familiar imagry.

As long as we can discover new ways to use it.

Original problem:
logo for a film.

Problem redefined:
make a connection between an image and the title.

Problem:
logo for a company which can put anyone's photograph in any background of their choice.

Original problem:
illustration for a speedwriting course.

Problem redefined:
illustration of a *fast* pen.

The New York Art Director's Club elects a few designers and art directors into their Hall of Fame eve year.

When Carl Fischer, the president, asked me to design the announceme I immediately said that I would be happy to do so, provided Carl, one New York's greatest photographers, would shoot my idea.

Of course, at that point, I *had* no idea. But I knew that conceiving a solution using a Fischer photograph would be interesting.

For the announcement of this prestigious event, I designed a flyer with a corny clip art illustration and very ordinary typography.

I made lots of xeroxes of the flyer or cheap paper.

I found a filthy, abandoned building and plastered the flyers on the wall, as rock bands, who can't afford pai advertising, do.

I then got Carl to photograph the wall, warts and all. His photograph became the announcement.

Problem:
poster for a nostalgic doo-wop music
about an amateur garage band.

First, I designed a leaflet loaded wi
clichés such as stars and musical
notes, etc., which looked as if the
band did it themselves.

I rented a fifties convertible and
put the leaflet under the windshield
wiper. And that became the final
poster.

And then I suggested to the produc
that he print one hundred thousand
leaflets so that he could have them
put under the windshield wipers of
every car within a hundred miles of
the theater.

Can you imagine? He refused.

Did I say there's no such thing as a
bad client? Of course there is.

As the American invasion of Iraq w
imminent, I modified the dove of
peace cliché on a holiday card to
express the way I felt.

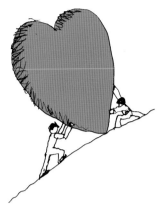

An illustration for a comedy about a love affair plagued with problems.

Even the daddy of all clichés, can *still* be used in a fresh way.

The cliché, "from soup to nuts" inspired this ad which implies that the film production company has a wide range of clients.

80

Take a statement like, "we cure cancer for a nickel." It isn't necessary to make a statement like that look interesting.

It *is* interesting.

If you are fortunate enough to work with interesting words, then let the words speak for themselves with the absolute minimum distraction from typography or color or layout.

If you try to make interesting words look interesting, the way they look competes with the statement.

There are thousands of images competing with your design for the audience's attention. If and when they get around to your design, make sure that the elements within your job don't compete with each other.

Although we will probably never have words as important as, "we cure cancer for a nickel," there will be words at times which should stand alone, unadorned.

**Live theater
is more exciting
than tv, movies
and sports.**

**Well, maybe
not sports.**

A booklet cover for a regional
theater in a town with a fanatical
devotion to sports. I wrote copy
which recognized the reality.

We
hate
small
print

Original problem:
booklet cover listing the rates of a
car rental company. (They boasted
that there's no *small print* in their
contracts.)

Problem redefined:
I exaggerated their boast on the
cover.

82

Bob Gill, formerly blah, blah, blah and blah,
blah, blah, blah, blah, blah, blah, blah, blah, blah.
Founded blah, blah, blah, blah, blah, blah,
blah, blah, blah, blah, blah, blah, blah, blah, blah,
blah, blah, blah, blah, blah, blah, blah, blah, blah.
blah, blah, blah, blah, blah, blah, blah, and blah.
He recently blah, blah, blah, blah, blah, blah.
blah, blah, blah, blah, blah, blah, blah, blah, blah.
Awarded a blah, blah, blah, blah, and blah.
blah, blah, blah, blah, blah, blah, blah, blah, blah.
He then blah, blah, blah, blah, blah, blah.
blah, blah, blah, blah, blah, blah, blah, blah, blah.
blah, blah, blah, blah, blah, blah, blah, and blah
blah, blah, blah, blah, blah, blah, blah, blah, blah.
blah, blah, is now available for design, illustration
and advertising projects at One Fifth Avenue,
New York, NY 10003. Telephone: (212) 460-0950
Fax: 646-602-6291 email: bobgilletc@nyc.rr.com

Original problem:
mailing piece to look for assignmen

Problem redefined
say you're terrific without saying it.

> GOING TO SEE THE
> SOUTH AFRICAN
> 'WHITES ONLY'
> CRICKET TEAM?
>
> (IT'S NOT CRICKET.)

Original problem:
poster to boycott a cricket match in London.

Problem redefined:
"it's not cricket," is an expression meaning, "it's not fair."

A friend asked me to design his party invitation. I explained that if there was something *special* that he could say about the party, it would give me an excuse to do something *special* with the invitation.

"Nothing special about the party," he said, "but could you ask everyone to bring a bottle."

Problem:
party invitation which *blackmails* guests into bringing a bottle.

> **Dear Friends:**
>
> John Cole invites you to a party on Sat. Sept. 9 at 8.30pm at 122 Regents Park Rd. NW1 Flat D. RSVP GRO 2291
>
> Please bring a bottle.

> **Free Loaders:**
>
> John Cole invites you to a party on Sat. Sept. 9 at 8.30pm at 122 Regents Park Rd. NW1 Flat D. RSVP GRO 2291

84

As I said, some words are so interesting, they need no embellishment.

However, in other cases, it's useful to know that letterforms can do more than just spell words.

A word, or even a letterform can *also* be an image.

For example:

Original problem:
booklet cover for a company offering 20% off its service.

Problem redefined:
take 20% off its name.

Original problem:
masthead for an anti-apartheid newspaper.

Problem redefined:
communicate the emotion associated with the word.

Original problem:
logo for John Page, sound recordist.

jŏn paj sownd

Problem redefined:
spell the client's name phonetically.

I couldn't decide where to put the three words on my own book jacket.

Even indecision can inspire a fresh image.

In this logo for Associates & Ferren, although I was asked to do an A & F, I thought it would be more interesting to show how the A & F was related to the name.

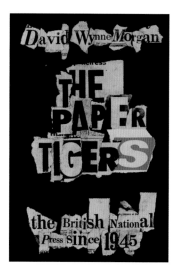

As the subject of this book was the press, I limited myself to elements torn from newspapers in this collage.

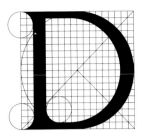

A logo inspired by the very precise intensive care monitoring equipment that the company makes.

Bob Gill represented by Bob Gore

An announcement of a connection between two people whose last names both begin with a G.

Rent a New Yorker

Original problem:
logo for a company which supplies guides to tourists.

RentaNooYawka

Problem defined:
as most guides are out-of-work actors from Ohio, give the company an accent so as to communicate that their guides are *authentic* New Yorkers.

FREESTYLE

Logo for a film comedy about hijink[s] on the ski slopes. In this case, the cliché of snow on letterforms does justice to the film, which is also a cliché.

ALICE IN WONDERLAND

Who could resist having the title of this theatrical version of "Alice" backwards every time the name wa[s] mentioned; on the cover of the playbill, on tickets, on ads, on posters, and even on the theater marquee.

A film comedy logo illustrating itself[.]

Another example of a film comedy logo illustrating itself.

A "D" with computer code for a data processing company…

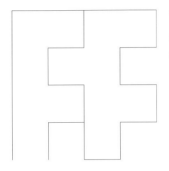

"FF" based on a grid of sixteen squares for a modular furniture company…

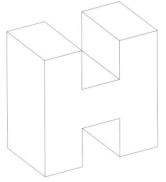

and an "H" drawn isometrically, for an architect.

10. On the other hand...

Did I say, "stick to reality?"

I also said, "don't listen to me, unless it's really helpful."

Reality, most of the time, is the way to go, for all of the reasons mentioned earlier in this book.

Truth, generally, is best illustrated with real images. But sometimes an impossible image can be more truthful than a real image.

For example:

Problem:
illustration about smoking a pipe gives a person an elegant persona.

Problem:
illustration about the deterioration of teenage academic standards.

I had a high school chair built that was one and a half times the size of a regular one.

Impossible images

When I asked the director what hi
musical was about, he said,"pure
dancing."

I went to a few rehearsals, made so
sketches and decided to combine
several dances and costumes into o
impossible image, opposite.

Jules Fisher, The Shubert Organization & Columbia Pictures present

Dancin'

a new musical entertainment
directed & choreographed by Bob Fosse

gill

Music and Lyrics by
Johann Sebastian Bach, George M. Cohan,
Neil Diamond, Bob Haggart & Ray Bauduc,
Jerry Leiber & Mike Stoller, Johnny Mercer &
Harry Warren, Louis Prima, Carol Bayer Sager
& Melissa Manchester,
Barry Mann & Cynthia Weil,
Erik Satie, John Philip Sousa,
Cat Stevens, Edgard Varèse, Jerry Jeff Walker.

Broadhurst Theatre
235 West 44th Street, New York, New York 10036

photo: Jack Mitchell dye transfer: Gerry Wind & Assocs

Paradox

There are infinite ways to upset the reader's equilibrium. I like to try as many as possible.

One of the ways is with a paradoxic image...an image which contradicts itself.

Original problem:
A company which restores computer and donates them to charities and schools. They use the phrase, "a computer is a terrible thing to waste." They asked me to use it in an ad. My first reaction was that it sounded like a quotation.

"A computer is a terrible thing to waste."

"A computer is a terrible thing to waste."
William Shakespeare

94

Problem redefined:
who is the most amazing, wonderful important person to have originated the quotation?

Original problem:
book jacket and poster for the New York Art Directors Annual Exhibition.

Problem redefined:
capture the irony of art directors givi each other medals, while at the same time, they wish each other dead. (Their rivalry is intense.)

65th
Art
Directors
Annual

A. JAIME

JAIME ASSOCIATES
STANDARD GRAPHIC DESIGN

527 MADISON AVE.
NEW YORK CITY 10022
(212) 832-9047

A. JAIME

JAIME ASSOCIATES
THE USUAL TYPESETTING

527 MADISON AVE.
NEW YORK CITY 10022
(212) 832-9047

A. JAIME

JAIME ASSOCIATES
VERY ORDINARY PHOTOSTATS

527 MADISON AVE.
NEW YORK CITY 10022
(212) 832-9047

A. JAIME

JAIME ASSOCIATES
AVERAGE PASTE-UP & MECHANICALS

527 MADISON AVE.
NEW YORK CITY 10022
(212) 832-9047

Original problem:
business card for a small studio.

When I asked them what exactly did they do. They said, "nothing very special. Typesetting, stats, newsletters, paste-ups and mechanicals."

I tried to make something special out of "nothing very special."

Problem redefined:
four business cards, accordion folded.

Original problem:
illustration for an advertising agency ad that promises never to do boring theater advertising.

Problem redefined:
how can the most boring words be made interesting?

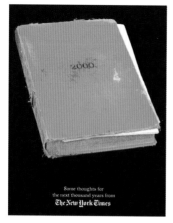

A paradoxical diary consisting of the ideas of some of the world's m important thinkers, arranged in pa which contradict each other, illustra with contradictory images.

Some thoughts for
the next thousand years from
The New York Times

"Some things have to be seen to be believed."
S. Harwood

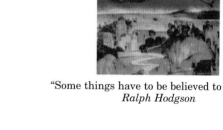

"Some things have to be believed to be seen."
Ralph Hodgson

"Why climb a Mountain? Because it is there."
George Mallory

"Why do writers write? Because it isn't there."
Thomas Bertger

"Love thy neighbor as thyself."
Genesis xix:18

"Kindness is in our power, but fondness is not."
Euripides

"Seek simplicity and distrust it."
Alfred North Whitehead

"Less is more."
Robert Browning

"Beauty is truth, truth beauty."
John Keats

"Beauty is in the eye of the beholder."
Hume

"Spare the rod, spoil the child."
Aelfric

"If you must beat a child, us a string."
The Talmud

"That's one small step for man,
one giant step for mankind."
Neil Armstrong (on landing on the moon)

"If you go expressly to look at the moon,
it becomes tinsel."
Alfred North Whitehead

An advertising agency wanted to project a new image, when they added a new partner. At the same time, they wanted to communicate they had been around for a long time.

As a way of giving them the identi of a new/old agency, I combined new/old architectural elements.

Original problem:
poster for a play about the Nazi occupation of Paris in WWII.

Problem redefined:
use the iconic, very moving photograph of a Frenchman reactir to the columns of German troops marching into Paris, as a way of illustrating the paradoxical title.
Opposite.

Good

Abstractions

Sometimes, when a problem involve
an abstract subject; truth, idealism,
creativity, love, etc., as it is difficult
use a specific image, the solution, li
the problem, is often abstract.

A specific image, say, a banana, is
perceived by everyone in the same
way. Everyone sees it as a banana

The obvious difficulty with an abstra
image, is that not everyone perceive
it in the *same* way. And, of course,
is harder to get a client to accept it.
Especially, which is often the case, i
the client shows it to half a dozen
colleagues, and he gets half a doze
interpretations.

But assuming an abstract image is
eventually accepted, as long as it is
perceived by everyone as interesting
and of high quality, even though no
everyone sees it the same way, that'
okay.

For example:

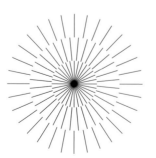

A logo for an entertainment
lighting company which tries to
express light glowing.

The Creative Network is a social/business group that's well named. Under thirties in dot coms, in advertising, and in design, exchange business cards and network, with a vengeance.

To me, networking is like dropping a pebble in a pool of water.

Letterheads, business cards, etc. all carry the concentric circles.

Logo for a *think tank*, with the company name halfway up the steps. Shown: die-cut upper left-hand corner of letterhead and business card, actual size.

As I said to the client, "although you're not yet at the ultimate solution to the problem that you're working on, you're well on the way."

Incidentally, while I'm on the subject of abstraction, I am reminded of an experience that I had in Germany while visiting the new Bauhaus, the design school in Ulm.

The director at the time, Moldinado, a South American architect, after a devastating criticism of my work, tried to straighten me out.

"Graphic design," he pontificated, either image or icon or noise."

"I know what image is," I said. "B can't the image be a drawing?"

"Absolutely not, a photograph is th only image of our time," he said.

"I know that an icon is a symbol. But noise," I said, "what's noise?

Moldinado unrolled some posters. "This is noise," he said, as he revealed the work of one of the instructors, Otl Aicher. They were announcements of university lecture

One, with a blue triangle, announce a lecture about *the tragedies of Shakespeare*. Another with angular shapes in black and white, announc *the origins of biology*. All of the posters consisted of abstract compositions.

"But," I said, "none of these posters have anything to do with the subjec of the lectures."

"Exactly," he said, "that's why it's called noise." It just attracts attentio

I raced back to London and the nex job that came along, I tried to make noise. I tried green parallel lines an then, blue squares. I couldn't decid whether the noise was any good. It was much too arbitrary for me.

That was the last time I tried.

102

Olympischer Sommer

A poster by Aicher for the 1972 Olympics held in Munich designed several years after my visit to Ulm.

Equinox: the precise time when the sun crosses the equator, making day and night, everywhere, of equal length.

Equinox is also the name of a film production company that needed a logo.

Solution:
left side of all items of stationery; letterhead, business card, memo, etc.

Logo for a series of radio programs on *what it means to be jewish.*

As there are as many versions of practicing Judaism as there are Jews. I thought the maze was the right way to represent the subject's intricacies.

Original problem:
cover for a white paper sample booklet.

Problem redefined:
how can a sheet of white paper seem more desirable than another sheet of white paper where it is impossible to tell the difference?

Solution:
I drew a sheet of white paper.

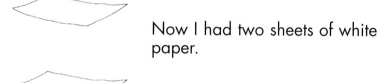

As it is virtually impossible to tell th difference between two quality she of white paper, I went to the extren and xeroxed my drawing so that I had an identical copy.

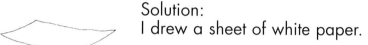

Now I had two sheets of white paper.

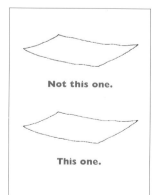

Not this one.

This one.

Although the two sheets were identical, I wrote some copy which *implied* that my client's paper was better than the competition's.

Problem:
book jacket.

I began with a maze which was both graphic *and* difficult.

Then I extended the maze to the back of the jacket, so that the back, when joined to the front, makes an image twice as wide.

And then, if another back was joined to the other side of the front, the image becomes three times as wide, and so on…

In my first year of art school, I was made aware of the surrealism of Magritte. I knew instantly, that I always would feel more connected to his work than to the work of any other creative person.

Ceci n'est pas une pipe.
(This is not a pipe.)
1928-1929
Collection: William N. Copley, New York.

I remember feeling that if I had been introduced to his work just a few years earlier, the course of my life would have changed. I would have become a painter, instead of a designer. I wonder, occasionally, if it would have resulted in a more satisfying life, or the opposite.

The rapport I still feel with him, and his work, although we never met, is as strong today, as it was over fifty years ago.

I am still fascinated by his appearance and his lifestyle. He looks more like an accountant, than a painter in his conventional blue suit, in his suburban house.

La lunette d'approche
(The Field Glass)
1963
Collection: Menil Foundation, Houston, Texas

I'm positive that his imagry has *absolutely* no symbolic meaning. He paints strange juxtapositions simply because he *feels like it*.

That's what fascinates me about him, more than anything else, his courage to paint things which cannot be justified, or explained.

In thinking about Magritte, a numb
of other creative people who I
admire, come to mind; especially
designers and illustrators whose
process is so different from mine.

Muller-Brockmann, is the
quintessential Swiss designer.

He loves every typeface, as long a
it is Helvetica Medium, and every
color as long as it is a warm red.

I have never seen a job of his that
isn't *perfect*. Perfect, in the
sense that the the placement of eve
element in the layout is so carefully
thought out; the "F" in *Film* which
overlaps the "e" and "r" in *der*.

You couldn't move these letterforms
centimeter.

Saul Steinberg is someone else wh
I admire so much. But in a totally
different way.

His wit goes so perfectly with his
whimsical drawing style.

Another thing about Steinberg that
I find so interesting is that he has th
foreigner's sense of wonder and
discovery about American images,
that natives never seem to notice.

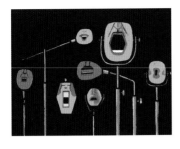

Another great wit is the French poster designer, Savignac.

I'm always so conscious of the fun he seems to have while making a living.

It's so interesting to compare his apparently free-wheeling process to Muller-Brockmann's highly controlled one.

They couldn't appear to be more different, and yet they both exude a supreme confidence.

If David Carson didn't exist, we'd have to invent him.

The time is long overdue for a radical new approaches to design and typography, as the present generation seems incabable of pushing the present aesthetic much further.

Whether we like it or not, design is subject to the whims of fashion.

However, it is also true that the more fashionable something is, the more likely it is to date.

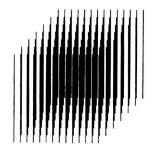

Karel Martens, the Dutch designer produces wonderfully *loud* noise.

(The description of *my* failure to make noise is on page 102.)

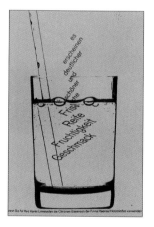

Karl Gerstner, Swiss, is another designer whose typographic eye is among the most elegant, and highly developed in the world.

Another interesting thing about Gerstner is how he goes from his commercial jobs to his fine art projects and back to his commercial jobs so effortlessly.

Franco Grignani, an Italian, has a design philosophy diametrically opposed to mine.

Grignani does the same thing, more or less, for every job.

He *knows* precisely what good design should look like. As I've said, ad infinitum, I *don't* believe in design absolutes.

But, in spite of everything, I respond to his very exciting shapes and patterns. (His *good design*.)

Am I contradicting myself? Absolutely.

Bruno Munguzzi, Swiss, is another favorite of mine. The obvious pleasure he derives from pushing type around, also gives *me* pleasure.

Ironically, anyone who has ever been a student of mine, will recall that *pushing type around* was always the worst thing I could say about their job.

But that's only because I wanted my students to experience having something interesting to say, rather than simply doing what they thought was an interesting layout, with no particular idea.

Obviously, it would be very boring if *all* designers pushed type around and made noise or if *all* designers were as obsessional as I am about trying to get an interesting idea.

112

12. Coda

Theory:

Earlier, I referred to the relationship between designer and client...

Designer and client agree on a problem. Usually boring.

Designer goes away, does the appropriate research, and redefines the problem, so that it is interesting, without changing the client's statement.

Eventually, the designer presents his solution.

Practice:

An ad for a film with an ironic title– that justice is *not* for all, but only for the rich.

Solution: justice defiled.

The producers hated it. They felt it wasn't commercial.

I got the model back, this time in a whore's outfit.

Solution:
justice can be bought.

Again, the producers hated it.

"Okay," I said, "what do you really want?"

"Don't give us justice," they said, "give us Al. Al Pacino sells tickets. Not justice."

Eventually, I made another presentation.

Needless to say, they hated that too. And then, they got rid of me.

Logo for a provincial theater company. The first one was inspired by a piece of scenery.

The client said that professional companies like theirs don't use flats. "Too amateurish," they said.

My mistake.

The second try was inspired by the glamor of the theater.

They hated it. They said, "too glamorous."

Another try:

This time inspired by theatrical lighting.

"Sorry," they said, "too dramatic," and they got rid of me.

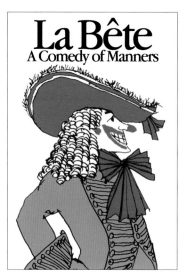

A poster for a farce about an eighteenth-century pompous fool.

Solution:
a clown.

The producer hated it. He said it wasn't commercial.

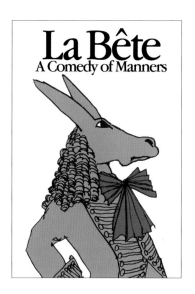

Another solution:
an ass.

He hated it.

The third try: making the character into a fool, without showing him.

The producer hated this one, too.

(The Schmuck)

I then translated the French title of the play, which was playing to an American audience, into Yiddish.

The producer hated this too, and he got rid of me.

Please don't think that I'm ending th
book on a bleak note, although
the last ten jobs shown; three for the
Pacino film, three for a provincial
theater and four for *La Bête*, were a
rejected.

If the clients had continued to put up
with me, I would have been happy
present an *infinite* number of solutio

One at a time, of course. I may thir
of many solutions, or do many
variations of the same solution, but,
the end, I only show what I think is t
best one each time.

**No matter how many times your
brilliant, amazing work is rejected fo
whatever arbitrary, dopey, frivolous
reason, there is always another
brilliant, amazing solution possible.**

I promise you.

118

120

13. Collaborators, clients, bio

Description	Client	Collaborators	Pa...
1			
Trade ad: *Nomads*	Elliot Kastner	Photo: Marty Jacobs	
Change of address card	Fishko/Gill		
Poster: Mother's Day	Abraham & Strauss	Photo: Marty Jacobs	
Readership survey	*The Learning Annex*	Photo: Marty Jacobs	
Logo	Radio Foundation		
House of Bernada Alba	Great Neck Theatre		
Trade ad illustration	*TV Guide*		
Holiday collage	Great Amer. Backrub		
Montage	Kate Gill	Photos: unknown	
Portrait of his mother	J. MacNeil Whistler		
Mother's Day illustration	*The New Yorker* *		
Diary illustrations	*The New York Times*		
Bottles	White Horse Whisky	Photos: John Summerhayes	
2 mailers	Bob Gill		
2			
Comic book illustration	Unknown	Artist unknown	2
Moving announcement	Forum Gallery	Photo: S. Parik	2
Logo	Conference Bureau		2
Logo	CommunityCartography	Redrawn by Jack Gill	2
Pencil sharpener	*American Artist* magazine		2
Pencil (two plays)	Tina Ball		2
3			
*Forget all the rules...*cover	Watson Guptil Publishing	Photo: Marty Jacobs	2
Logo: *Horowitz*	Joel Shanker	Lettering: George Hoy	3
4			
Logo	Aeronautical & General Model Makers	Photo: John Summerhayes	3
Logo: *Dangerous Games*	Jules Fisher	Photo: Marty Jacobs	4
Poster: *Total Abandon*	Elizabeth McCann		4
4 Seasonal logos	Lake Sagamore Ass.		4
4 logos	The Tie Shop*		4
Season's Greetings	Bob Gill		4
Letterhead	Fishko/Gill	Redrawn by Jack Gill	4
Book cover	*Penrose Annual*	Photo: John Summerhayes	4
Record Sleeve	Troubadour Records	Photo: John Summerhayes	4
Bob & Ray microphones	Radio Foundation	Retouching: Wolf Spoerl	4
Bob & Ray photo	Radio Foundation	Photo: unknown	4
Queen Elizabeth illustration	*The Learning Annex*	Photo: unknown	4
Philistines poster	Alberta College of Art	Photo: Marty Jacobs	4
Rock 'n Roll poster	Jules Fisher	Robert Rabinowitz Photo unknown Retoucher: Ram	4
Jazz illustration	*Queen* magazine		4
Bridges logo	Radio Foundation		4
Night scene illustration	Datascope, Inc.	Photo: Marty Jacobs	4
Traffic illustration	*Fortune*		5
Information highway cover	Women's Advertising Club		5
Logo	Steve Baum Productions		5

Description	Client	Collaborators	Page
Broom illustration	*The Learning Annex*		51
2 left feet illustration	*Nova* magazine		51
Hair calendar	Robert Norton Associates	Photo: John Summerhayes	52
Moving announcement.	Bob Gill		52
Football illustration	*The New Yorker**		53

5

Logo	Television Associates		55
Logo	Fucci/Stone, Inc.		55
Chorus of Disapproval logo	Elliott Kastner	Photo: Unknown	56
U.N. lunch	United Nations Ass.		56
Working at home	*The Learning Annex*		57
With God on Our Side ad	Lumiere Productions		57
British packaged goods	British Board of Trade	Redrawn by Jack Gill	58
Ecumenical card	Bob Gill		58
Drinks logo	Name withheld by request*		59
Fundraising booklet cover	Indiana Repertory Theatre		59
Logo: *Private Secretary*	CBS Television		59
Ad	El Al Israel Airlines	Photo: John Cole	60
Logo: *Julius Caesar*	Elliott Kastner	Photo: John Summerhayes	60
Three-man exhibition	The Photographers Gallery		61
Poster	School of Visual Arts	Photo: Ronnie Rojas	61
Poster: *Go Between*	EMI Films	Photo: unknown	61
Telephones	Geers Gross Advertising		62
Police	Geers Gross Advertising		62
Ad: *This is a winter coat*	El Al Israel Airlines	Photo: John Cole	63
Poster: *Requiem…*	Zeff Buffman	Photo: Marty Jacobs	63

6

Logo: *Divorce*	The Mermaid Theatre	A. Fletcher & C. Forbes	65
Invoice	Bob Gill	Redrawn by Jack Gill	66
55	Victor Herbert		66
From/to	Cystic Fibrosis Foundation		67
Announcement	Kynock Press		67
Posters	*Evening Standard*	A. Fletcher & C. Forbes	68
Gift certificate image	Great American Backrub		68
Playing card	Langen & Wind		68
4 ads	D&AD Ass.		69
Writing project logo	Equinox Films		70
Annual Report covers	*The Learning Annex*	Photos: Marty Jacobs	70/71

7

Logo	MG Productions		73
Christmas card	Bob Gill		74
Cheap thrill ad	*The Learning Annex*		74
Logo booklet cover	Bob Gill		74
Human Language logo	Equinox Films		75
Logo	Imagine Yourself, Inc.		75
Speed writing illustration	*The Learning Annex*		75
Hall of Fame poster	NY Art Directors Club	Photo: Carl Fischer	77
Forever Plaid poster	Gene Wolsk	Photo: Marty Jacobs	78
Crying dove	Bob Gill		78

Description	Client	Collaborators	Pag
Logo: *The Sum of Us*	Grey Entertainment Adv.		7
Soup to nuts ad	MG Productions		7
8			
Booklet cover	Indiana Repertory Theater		8
We hate small print cover	Martins Car Rental		8
Cricket poster	Anti-Apartheid movement		8
Party invitation	John Cole		8
			8
9			
20% off booklet cover	Martins Car Rental		8
Newspaper masthead	Anti-Apartheid movement		8
Logo	John Page Sound		8
Bob Gill Portfolio cover	Lund Humphries, Ltd.		8
Logo	Associates & Ferren	Redrawn by Jack Gill	8
Paper Tigers cover	Anthony Blond, Ltd.		8
Logo	Datascope, Inc.	Lettering: Ozzie Greif	8
Announcement	Bob Gore	Redrawn by Jack Gill	8
Logo: *Freestyle*	Columbia Pictures		8
Logo: *Alice in Wonderland*	Nappi/Eliran Advertising		8
Logo: *Casey's Shadow*	Columbia Pictures		8
Logo: *Mummy*	Elliott Kastner		8
Logo	Datum Group	Redrawn by Jack Gill	8
Logo	Formation Furniture, Ltd.	Redrawn by Jack Gill	8
Logo	Brian Harvey, architect	Redrawn by Jack Gill	8
10			
Illustration: pipe smoker	*Nova* magazine		9
Illustration: student	*Time*	Photo: Marty Jacobs	9
Poster: *Dancin'*	Jules Fisher	Photo: Jack Mitchel	9
		Retouching: Bernie Wolsk	
Computer headline	Steve Baum Productions		9
Poster/cover	NY Art Directors Club	Photo: Marty Jacobs	9
		Retouching: Bernie Wolsk	
Business card	Al Jaime		9
Theater image	Nappi/Eliran Advertising		9
Diary	*The New York Times*	Photos: various	96/9
New/old ad agency	Name withheld by request	Photos: Tara Studios	9
Poster: *Good*	Nappi/Eliran Advertising	Photo: unknown	9
Logo	Third Eye		10
Logo	The Creative Network		10
Letterhead	Applied Minds, Inc.		10
Logo	Equinox Films		10
Logo: *What is a Jew?*	Radio Foundation		10
Booklet cover	Strathmore Paper Co.		10
Cover: *Graphic Design Made Difficult*	Van Nostrand Reinhold		10

Description	Client	Collaborators	Page
12			
Ads: *And Justice for All*	Columbia Pictures*	Photo: Marty Jacobs	113/114
Logos	Indiana Rep. Theatre*		115
Posters: *La Bête*	Grey Entertainment*		116/117
13			
Leaflet	Mexican American Workers Association	Retouching: Jack Gill	128

Alphabetical Client List

Abraham & Strauss 12
AGM 39
Alberta College of Art 47
Amer. Artist magazine 23
Anthony Blond Ltd. 78
Anti-Apartheid Movement 83, 85
Applied Minds, Inc. 101
Associates & Ferren 86
Tina Ball 23
Steve Baum Productions 50, 94
Anthony Blond, Ltd. 86
British Board of Trade 58
Zeff Buffman 63
CBS Television 59
John Cole 83
Columbia Pictures 88, 113*, 114*
CommunityCartography 23
Conference Bureau 22
The Creative Network 101
Cystic Fibrosis Foundation 67
D&AD Ass. 69
Datascope, Inc. 49, 87,
Datum Group 89
El Al Israel Airlines 60, 63
EMI Films 53
Equinox Films 70, 75, 103
Evening Standard 68
Jules Fisher 40, 47, 93
Fishko/Gill 8, 44
Forum Gallery 22

Formation Furniture 89
Fortune 50
Fucci/Stone, Inc. 55
Geers Gross Advertising 62
Bob Gill 19, 43, 52, 66, 74, 79, 82, 86
Kate Gill 14
Bob Gore 87
Great Amer. Backrub 14, 68
Great Neck Theatre 13
Grey Entertainment 79*, 116*, 117*
Brian Harvey 89
Victor Herbert 66
Imagine Yourself, Inc. 75
Indiana Repertory Theatre 59, 82, 115*
Al Jaime 95
Elliott Kastner 8, 48, 56, 60, 88
Kynock Press 67
Lake Sagamore Ass. 42
Langen & Wind 68
Lawyer magazine 100
The Learning Annex 12, 46, 51, 70, 71, 74, 75
Lumiere Productions 49
Lund Humphries, Ltd. 78
Martins Car Rental 82, 85
Elizabeth McCann 41
Mermaid Theatre 65
Mexican American Workers Association 128
MG Productions 73, 79

Nappi Eliran Advertising 88, 95, 99*
The New Yorker 16*, 53*
Robert Norton Ass. 52
Nova magazine 51, 91
NY Art Directors Club 77, 94
The New York Times 17, 96, 97
John Page Sound 85
Penrose Annual 45
The Photographers Gallery 61
Queen magazine 100
Radio Foundation 13, 46, 48, 103
RentaNooYawka 87
School of Visual Arts 61
Joel Shanker 32
Strathmore Paper Company 104
Television Associates 55
The Tie Shop 42*
Third Eye 100
Time 91*
Troubadour Records 45
TV Guide 13
United Nations Ass. 56
Van Nostrand Reinhold 105
Watson Guptil Publishing 27
White Horse Whisky 18
Gene Wolsk 70
Women's Advertising Club 50

Jobs rejected by the client are indicated by*

126

Bob Gill

Bob Gill is a designer, an illustrator, a copywriter, a film-maker and a teacher.

After freelancing in New York, he went to London on a whim in 1960 and stayed 15 years. He started Fletcher/Forbes/Gill, a design office with the two brightest designers in England.

F/F/G began with two assistants and a secretary. Today, it's called *Pentagram,* with offices everywhere except Tibet.

Gill resigned in 1967 to work independently in London.

He returned to New York in 1975 to write and design *Beatlemania*, the largest multimedia musical up to that time on Broadway, with Robert Rabinowitz, the painter.

Gill still works independently and still teaches. He's had one-man shows in Europe, South America, the Far East and in the US.

He was elected to the New York Art Directors Club Hall of Fame and the Designers and Art Directors Association of London recently presented him with their Lifetime Achievement Award.

This is his sixth book about design and illustration. He's also written and illustrated a number of children's books.

He's now living in New York with his wife, New York Public Radio's Sara Fishko, their son, Jack, and their daughter, Kate.

128

If I show my face, I'll be fired.
**Please help me. My name is Carlos.
I work 12 hours a day, 6 days a week
for $2.60 an hour. I get no health
benefits and no respect. Thousands
of workers like me in greengroceries
are desperate to unionize.**
Here's what you can do: **talk to us about our conditions, honor
our boycotts, patronize union shops and telephone (212) 860-6705
Sponsored by Mexican American Workers Association.
Local 169, Box No. 79, 151 First Avenue, New York, NY 10003**